AMERICAN DREAM
A Journey With Some American Saints

CREATED BY A GROUP OF UNIVERSITY STUDENTS AND PROFESSORS
FROM THE UNITED STATES, CANADA, AND SWITZERLAND

EDITED BY STEPHEN E. LEWIS
GRAPHIC DESIGN BY ALYSSA STORM

ISBN: 9781941457047
Human Adventure Books
Tampa, 2017

HAB
HUMAN ADVENTURE BOOKS

*Saints, in a very real sense, do not give up something
for Christ but want Christ, desire the event of Christ
so much that their whole lives become permeated by that
event, even visibly, even in the form that their lives take:
the renunciation is only an apparent mode.*

LUIGI GIUSSANI

AMERICAN DREAM
A JOURNEY WITH SOME AMERICAN SAINTS

CREATED BY A GROUP OF UNIVERSITY STUDENTS AND PROFESSORS
FROM THE UNITED STATES, CANADA, AND SWITZERLAND

EDITED BY STEPHEN E. LEWIS
GRAPHIC DESIGN BY ALYSSA STORM

INTRODUCTION

American Dream: A Journey With Some American Saints is a voyage in the company of a group of American saints through space and time, criss-crossing the immense North American continent and extending across four centuries. The exhibit was created by a group of university students and professors from the United States, Canada, and Switzerland who, out of an interest in understanding what holiness amounts to, studied the lives and works of a selection of saints from North America. Our reading and discussion brought us to a better knowledge of our own history, and of our very selves. The exhibit's title *American Dream* is intended to be provocative: we aim to show that running through the history of North America are the stories of men and women who dreamed of bringing Jesus to this land, and who, by doing so, began to build up a new humanity.

Several important themes appear as one moves through the exhibit. In the course of their missions, all of the saints whose lives we present encountered men and women who were very different from themselves. Indeed, their zeal to communicate the Good News led these saints to make often astounding efforts to understand and embrace the other.

Another significant characteristic of these saints is their humanity. The exhibit depicts them as they are given to us through the historical sources, as products of their time, full of limits and contradictions, but also as individuals embarked on gradual paths of conversion, experiencing personal dramas, and enduring significant hardships. Each human detail renders more and more evident the exceptionality of their witness, and encourages us to ask questions about the source of their strength. Finally, there is the discovery that, in reading the lives and letters of these saints, their initial distance from us, due to language, culture, and sensibilities so often different from our own habits of thinking, gives way to a surprising sense of familiarity. They have become our travelling companions, and the Church, in canonizing them in recent times, has suggested that their witness has a value for the contemporary world. This leads us to ask: What do these saints have to say to us today?

This journey offers four presentations of the lives of saints who lived from the seventeenth through the twentieth centuries, and, in a concluding section, offers a glimpse of some of the fruits of their vocations.

***

This booklet is the transcript of the exhibit "American Dream" that was presented in August 2016 at the Meeting for Friendship among Peoples in Rimini, Italy, and in January 2017 at the New York Encounter, in New York City. We are grateful to the more than one hundred people all over the world who have contributed to this project.

Thanks to: Dr. Stephanie Morris, director of the Sisters of the Blessed Sacrament Archive, Bensalem, PA; Fr. David P. Reid, SSCC, Postulator for the cause of canonization of Damien de Veuster; Rubén Mendoza; Rose Marie Beebe and Robert M. Senkewicz; and Santiago Ramos.

I.
THE JESUIT
NORTH AMERICAN MARTYRS

North American Martyrs,
1642-1649

Our journey begins in New France, the region of North America colonized by the French from the sixteenth through the eighteenth centuries. From 1642 to 1649, eight French Jesuits who had ventured to New France following the great tradition of their spiritual fathers, Ignatius of Loyola and Francis Xavier, would die martyrs in the course of the war that raged between two native tribes, the Hurons and the Iroquois. In this section, we present the lives of three of these eight martyrs: Jean de Brébeuf, Isaac Jogues, and Charles Garnier.

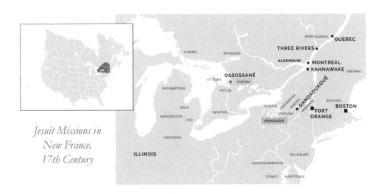

Jesuit Missions in
New France,
17th Century

The colonization of New France was extremely difficult, with several failed attempts to establish settlements. The land was terribly inhospitable, eliciting from no less than Jacques Cartier, the French explorer who discovered it, the description of the region as "the land God gave to Cain." In contrast, the Jesuit Charles Garnier, speaking about the people and territory in his mission, saw something very different:

> *If to me Canada is a holy temple and a most sacred spot that God has built for me in this world, the Huron region is its holy of holies. This is the field from which our Fathers hope to reap the richest harvest of all the places where we are working.* [1]

Jacques Cartier, 1491-1557

Jean de Brébeuf (1593-1649) was the founder of the mission to the Hurons, the settlement-based people with whom the Jesuits succeeded in coming into contact. Brébeuf was a tall and robust man, and the Native Americans, struck by his strength, nicknamed him "The Big Tree." His letters reveal an extraordinary capacity to love, and attest to his great efforts to understand a group of human beings who were so different from him. We see in his letters that for a Jesuit missionary, it was essential to immerse oneself in the mission territory's culture.

> *We must have a sincere affection for the savages, looking on them as redeemed by the Blood of the Son of God, and as our brothers with whom we are to spend the rest of our lives.* [2]

Jean de Brébeuf, 1593-1649

At forty years of age, Brébeuf began to study the Huron language, aware that without being able to communicate with the natives it would be impossible to convert them. He would come to edit the first dictionary of the Huron language, and translate many Christian prayers and songs into Huron, making use of images and concepts that could be understood by the natives. In a letter to his Jesuit brothers, he described the special challenges of this intellectual work in a striking way:

> *You may have been a famous professor or an outstanding theologian in France, but here you will be merely a student and—God be praised!—with what teachers!—women, little children, all the savages. You will constantly be exposed to their ridicule. The Huron language will be your St. Thomas and your Aristotle, and—clever man that*

you are, speaking glibly among learned and capable persons—you must make up your mind to be for quite some time mute in the company of these barbarians. It will be quite an achievement if, at the end of a considerable time, you begin to stammer even a little. [3]

Brébeuf saw the sense of wonder that the Native Americans felt in front of the beauty of the universe as a bridge for discovering the one true God:

[The Hurons] have recourse to the Sky in almost all their necessities, and respect the great bodies in it above all creatures, and remark in it in particular something divine. Indeed, it is, after man, the most vivid image we have of Divinity; there is nothing which represents him to us so clearly; we remark his omnipotence in all the prodigious effects they cause here below, his immensity in their vast extent, his wisdom in the order of their movements, his goodness in the benign influences they shed continually over all creatures, and his beauty in the Sun and in the aspect of the Stars. I say this to show how easy it will be, with time and divine aid, to lead these Peoples to the knowledge of their Creator, since they already honor so especially a creature which is so perfect an image of him. [4]

Given all of the challenges of communication, Brébeuf's first converts were a miracle, and he was moved by their lives. He wrote the following about a Native American whom he baptized and who took the name of Joseph:

Some of our Frenchmen must here correct the notion they have had of our Savages, imagining them as ferocious beasts having nothing human about them save the exterior Formation of the body. [Joseph], whose heart God has touched, [...] is in no respect inferior to the most zealous Catholic of France.[...] His constancy in goodness has made him and all his family remarkable, not only to the people of the village, but also to the whole country, so that they talk about him very differently. The most reasonable have admired him, and are admiring him still more every day; others ridicule him. [5]

The Jesuits' efforts were made more difficult by the smallpox epidemic, which decimated the Huron populations during these years. Slowly, the not completely erroneous idea that the Europeans were the carriers of the epidemic spread among the Native American populations. The Jesuits stayed with the people in their sufferings, tending to the sick and burying the dead, and over time were able to gain their trust. Brébeuf wrote in one of his letters:

Our Fathers buried [the smallpox victim] with as much solemnity as they could. [One of the Indians], having seen all this, and also observing that we did not wish to accept any of the belongings or clothes of the deceased, which he offered us, was so pleased and astonished that he went about among the cabins of the Savages [...], relating all that he had seen, saying, that we had given the best food we had to this poor young man, that we had nursed him as if he had been our own brother [...]. Some of them were so touched by this, especially his own family, that they brought us his daughter, who had died in childbirth, to bury her in our way [...]. [6]

Another serious challenge to the missions was war. The Iroquois, armed by Dutch and English traders, were bitter enemies of the Hurons and their allies the French, and waged a bloody war against them which lasted for many years and resulted in the capture and death of many Hurons and Jesuit missionaries. When Brébeuf was captured by the Iroquois, his strength, indestructible hope, and ability to support his fellow prisoners with prayer and exhortation surprised and infuriated the Iroquois, who tortured him for a long time before killing him along with his companion Gabriel Lalemant.

Martyrdom of Jean de Brébeuf and Gabriel Lalemant, 1649

In order to keep him from talking, they cut off his lips and tongue and, as a sort of mock-baptism, poured boiling water over him. These are the words of some eyewitnesses:

> *Before their death, both their hearts were torn out, by means of an opening above the breast; and those Barbarians inhumanly feasted thereon, drinking their blood quite warm, which they drew from its source with sacrilegious hands. While still quite full of life, pieces of flesh were removed from their thighs, from the calves of the legs, and from their arms, which those executioners placed on coals to roast, and ate in their sight. They had slashed their bodies in various parts; and, in order to increase the feeling of pain, they had thrust into these wounds red-hot hatchets.* [7]

Isaac Jogues, 1607-1646

Isaac Jogues (1607-1646), whom we could call "the poet" of the group, was a mystic, capable of being spiritually moved by the beauty of nature. Some of his letters are truly poetic. The most precious witness he has left is contained in the letters he wrote to his mother, in which he expresses his enthusiasm for his calling. This is how he greeted her before departing for North America:

> *I am sure [...] that if you accept this little sorrow as you should, it will be an act extremely pleasing to God, since,*

for his love, not only would it be right for you to give one son, but all your other sons, and even life itself, should that be necessary. For a little worldly gain, some men cross the sea and endure at least as much as we do, but, for the love of God we are unwilling to offer what these men do for their worldly affairs. Farewell, my dearest Mother. Thank you for the great love you have always given me, and especially for the tender devotion shown at our last meeting. May God reunite us in his holy Paradise if we do not ever again see each other here on earth. [8]

Jogues' life in the mission was not easy, and despite his great efforts, conversions were few. This prompted him to reflect upon the meaning of his work:

Would not all the labors of a thousand men be well rewarded in the conversion of one single soul to Jesus Christ? [9]

Jogues was captured and imprisoned by the Iroquois for one year, during which he was enslaved and severely tortured. Despite his suffering, he decided to accept his imprisonment:

Although it is true that I could probably have escaped [...] I had decided that with the help of God's grace I would live and die on the cross to which our Lord had affixed me with himself. Indeed, if I should leave, who would console the French prisoners or absolve anyone who wished the sacrament of penance? Who would remind the baptized Huron captives of their duties, instruct the new prisoners who were continuously being brought in, baptize the dying, and support those agonizing in their torments? [10]

Jogues finally escaped, and was able to return to France, where he spent Christmas with his family. But his heart remained in New France, and he wished to return. He therefore accepted the opportunity to become French ambassador to the Iroquois, the people who had already once captured and tortured him.

My heart tells me that if I have the blessing of being sent on this mission, Ibo et non redibo: I shall go, and shall not return. I shall be happy if Our Lord wills to finish the sacrifice where he began it. May the little blood that I shed in that land be a pledge of what I am willing to give him from all the veins of my body and from my heart. Indeed, that nation is as "a spouse of blood to me." [11]

Made prisoner and enslaved by the Iroquois once again, Jogues was eventually killed by the blow of an ax to the head.

Martyrdom of Isaac Jogues, 1646

7

The third Jesuit we encounter in our journey is Charles Garnier (1606-1649), a man with a complicated and dramatic story. His father, a secretary to the King, opposed his joining the Society of Jesus, and when he arrived in New France, he was for a long time troubled by the lack of conversions and by a sense of powerlessness. His early letters express a desire to accomplish heroic deeds, almost as if to redeem himself from his current failures. But with time, Garnier abandoned himself to God, the true source of hope.

Charles Garnier, 1606-1649

I pray to God—he wrote—to grant me two requests: First, that in every task I be able to remain united to him; and second, that I do not place any obstacle to that which he asks of me for the salvation of these poor people. [...] We can do absolutely nothing for the salvation of souls unless God is on our side. When we rely on him alone, through our obedience, he is obliged to help us. And with him, we accomplish all that he expects of us. On the other hand, when we ourselves choose our work, even though it be the holiest on earth, God has no obligation to give us aid. He leaves us to ourselves. [12]

Like his fellow Jesuits, Garnier did not flee from sacrifice. To his superior, who advised him to reflect about his own stay in hostile territory, he wrote:

What I fear more [than hunger] is leaving my flock in the time of their calamities and in the terrors of war—in a time when they need me more than ever. In such circumstances I am afraid I would fail to see the opportunities God gives me of losing my life for him [...]. [13]

Ultimately, Garnier was killed by the Iroquois when they raided the Huron-allied village where he was living. His life explains why what to the explorers looked like "the land of Cain" instead for Garnier and his fellow Jesuits never ceased being "the holiest place," which God had created for them. For the Jesuits, any place was a holy place for the task of fulfilling one's vocation, whether that involved being a missionary out in the wild, or teaching in a school in Europe. To young Jesuits in France who insisted on being sent to Canada, the superior of the Society suggested:

It is better, in my opinion, while one is still in France, not to think either of the Hurons, or of the Algonquins, or of the Montagnez, or of Kebec,

Martyrdom of Charles Garnier, 1649

or of Miskou, or even of converting the Savages, but to take up the Cross wherever Jesus Christ shall offer it to us. [14]

In a few years, the Iroquois wiped out the Hurons and completely destroyed the Jesuit missions. A few hundred surviving Huron converts were transferred to a safer place further north, near the French settlement of Montréal. The mission among the North American natives appeared to many to be a failure.

But how do we measure success? And what, in the depths of their hearts, were the first missionaries looking for? Instead of counting up results, the Jesuits saw the mission as an opportunity to know, follow, and love Christ, first and foremost for themselves. This is how Brébeuf would conclude his *Instructions* to the missionaries:

> *Jesus Christ is our true greatness; it is he alone and his crosses that should be sought in ministering to these people. If we seek for anything else, we will find nothing but bodily and spiritual afflictions. But if we have found Jesus Christ in his cross, we have found the roses among the thorns, sweetness in bitterness, everything in nothing at all.* [15]

As we shall see in the final section of this exhibit, time would reveal other unforeseen flowerings among the thorns, thus making Brébeuf, who wrote the following sentence, a prophet:

> *[…] never will this field produce fruit except through mildness and patience; for one should never expect to force it by violent and arbitrary action.* [16]

II.
JUNÍPERO SERRA

Now we move 3,000 miles west and one century forward, to a region called Alta and Baja California, which today runs through both the United States and Mexico, but which in the eighteenth century was under Spanish rule.

Alta & Baja California,
18th Century

Junípero Serra, 1713-1784
© Santa Bárbara Mission
Archive-Library

The subject of our story is Junípero Serra, a Spanish Franciscan who founded the first missions in Alta California and led the initial evangelization of the indigenous peoples of that land.

Established and well-regarded as a professor of theology at the University of Palma on the Spanish island of Majorca, Serra at age 35 asked to be allowed to go to the missions of New Spain. From then on he dedicated himself to proclaiming the Gospel in a way that was adapted to the particular culture of the indigenous peoples of California.

10

*Franciscan Missions in
California, 18th Century*

SAN FRANCISCO SOLANO: 1823
SAN RAFAEL ARCÁNGEL: 1817
SAN FRANCISCO DE ASÍS: 1776
SAN JOSÉ: 1797
SANTA CLARA DE ASÍS: 1777
SANTA CRUZ: 1791
SAN JUAN BAUTISTA: 1797
SAN CARLOS BORROMEO: 1770
SOLEDAD: 1791
SAN ANTONIO: 1771
SAN MIGUEL ARCÁNGEL: 1797
SAN LUIS OBISPO: 1772
LA PURISIMA CONCEPCIÓN: 1787
SANTA INÉS: 1804
SANTA BARBARA: 1786
SAN BUENAVENTURA: 1782
SAN FERNANDO: 1797
SAN GABRIEL ARCÁNGEL: 177
SAN JUAN CAPISTRANO: 17
SAN LUIS REY: 1798
SAN DIEGO: 1769

He personally baptized more than five hundred Native Americans, and he confirmed over five thousand. In the course of his work he travelled over 15,000 miles and founded nine missions in then-unexplored territory – among them San Diego de Alcalà and San Francisco de Asís, both of which are of course major cities today.

Serra's life complicates the standard history of the settlement of "America." His story reminds us that the exploration and colonization of North America was not solely the work of the Protestant Pilgrims who, fleeing persecution and the religious conflicts that were tearing Europe apart, settled along the east coast; nor was it simply a slow conquest, from east to west, motivated by the search for land and riches. Rather, it was also the adventure of missionaries who walked for thousands of miles, pushed by the desire to bring Christ to a people who at that point did not know Him. This is why Pope Francis recently referred to Serra as "one of the Founding Fathers of the United States," and why his statue was chosen by the citizens of California to represent the state in the National Statuary Hall in Washington, D.C. – a place which houses the statues of illustrious citizens from every state in the United States.

What motivated Serra to leave the land of his birth, his family, friends, and a brilliant academic career? Francisco Palóu, a fellow Franciscan missionary, writes that when Serra decided to leave:

*Statue of Junípero Serra, National
Statuary Hall, Washington, D.C.*

He rekindled in his heart those desires which had stirred him as a novice but which had become deadened because of his preoccupation with study. [18]

For the Spanish Franciscans, the opportunity to encounter and live among un-baptized people in New Spain—people whom Serra always referred to as "gentiles," never as "savages" or "wild Indians"—was an opportunity to live out a rigorous adherence to St. Francis of Assisi's apostolic way of life, and thus that of Christ.

A short time before leaving Spain, Serra wrote a long letter to his cousin, as he did not dare to tell his very old parents in person about his departure. He knew that he would probably never see them again.

This is a letter of farewell, since we are about to leave this city of Cádiz and sail to Mexico. [...] My beloved friend, I am at a loss for words, yet overwhelmed by emotion as I depart. I beg you once again to comfort my parents. I know they will be greatly affected by my leaving. I wish I could instill in them the great joy that I am experiencing because I believe they would urge me to go forth and never turn back. They should realize that the role of apostolic preacher is so much more when it is put into practice. This is the most they could hope for, that is, to see me fulfill my responsibilities well. [...]

Tell them I still feel badly that I am not able to stay in close proximity with them as I was before, in order to console them. But [...] our first obligation is to do the will of God and fulfill it. [...]

I remember when my father had that very serious illness, and they gave him the last rites. At that time I was already a religious and was attending to him, thinking that he was dying. When he and I were alone he told me, "My son, what I want from you is for you to be a good religious of the Padre San Francisco." Well, father, know that those words are never far from my thoughts, as if I heard you utter them at this very instant. And also know that I have undertaken this path to try to become a good religious. Do not feel sad, for I am doing as you wish, which also is the will of God. [20]

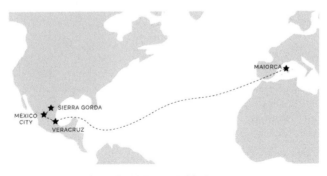

Serra's Journey to Mexico

Serra landed in the Mexican port of Veracruz and from there undertook a long and tiresome journey that brought him to Mexico City. But he would have to wait another eighteen years to be able, finally, in 1769, to depart for Alta California – a minimally-explored and unsettled land where Christianity was unknown. He was 55 years of age. The diary of his first expedition north among the "gentiles" testifies to Serra's enthusiasm and yearning to meet that un-baptized population.

> *Even though we have seen many Indians, we have not seen so many gathered together in one place as we have here. And as to their friendly nature, I cannot find the appropriate words to describe it. [...] One of the women wanted me to hold the infant she was nursing. I held him in my arms for a while, so wishing that I could baptize him, but I then returned the child to his mother.*

> *I make the sign of the cross and bless each of them. I have them say "Jesus and Mary." I give them what I am able to give and cherish them in the best way I can. We manage to get by like this since there is no other work we can do at the present time.* [21]

Mission San Gabriel, Ferdinand Deppe, c. 1832

The foundation of the missions allowed Serra and his fellow Franciscan friars to live among the natives and share life with them. The typical California mission was conceived as a right and proper village, where the local indigenous peoples were invited to live permanently. Generally, in Serra's time, the mission consisted of two Franciscans, six soldiers, one superintendent with a family, and around two hundred indigenous people.

The mission normally included numerous buildings, among which were workshops, storehouses, dormitories, offices, and a church. The surrounding land was used to teach the indigenous people about farming and the raising of livestock. The missionaries cultivated barley, maize, wheat, beans, and a wide variety of other crops and fruit. Wine production, which today has made California famous, began with the Franciscan missions because wine was required for the celebration of the Mass. The mission had to supply itself with food, as well as its presidio, where the soldiers were garrisoned.

A typical day in the mission included time set aside for work and time set aside for instruction, Mass, catechism, and the learning of sacred music. Although they had less expertise than the Jesuits, the Franciscans made great efforts to understand their native interlocutors, learn their languages, and come to know their traditions. Communication was always a significant challenge for Serra and his brethren.

> *The door is open for [this] work thanks to the interpreters, which we were lacking before. With the knowledge and help of the interpreters, the religious missionaries are beginning to learn the various languages. And I say various, because of the five missions which have been founded, and of those we expect to found soon, there are not even two missions where the same language is spoken.* [22]

The Franciscans made clever use of art and architecture in their efforts to communicate.

From the Doctrina Cristiana, Egerton MS 2898, fol. 1b. Museum Number: Am1962.03.213. © Trustees of the British Museum.

What you see here is the "Our Father" rendered in symbols and words, part of a Náhuatl catechism used by seventeenth-century Spanish missionaries to evangelize the Nahua people (the Aztecs). Serra and his brethren made similar efforts. Recent archaeological studies have revealed how the churches in the Franciscan missions were oriented when constructed to catch the light of the sun during specific days of the year – during festivals that were very important for the native population, as well as major Catholic feast days. [23]

Mission San Juan Bautista, Winter Solstice
© 2007 Rúben Mendoza.

Presidio Santa Bárbara, Winter Solstice
© 2008 Rúben Mendoza

This attests to an extraordinary effort to become familiar with local sensibilities. The beauty of the missions, which one can still admire today, testifies to the passion and love that the Franciscans had for the people whom they had encountered.

Notwithstanding all of these efforts, the Franciscans' understanding of the indigenous peoples was limited and their approach to them was sometimes paternalistic. The friars saw the California natives as their children, incapable of governing themselves and in need of guidance, protection, instruction, and discipline. This paternalism explains the use of corporal punishment by the missionaries – a controversial topic that has often prompted a negative view and interpretation of Serra and his companions' missions. However, corporal punishment was in that period a normal practice in Europe, so the missionaries were not subjecting the native Californians to something that they themselves were not subject to. The real issue was again that of communication, for a punishment is only effective if the one being punished understands why. Serra was always concerned for the welfare of the native Californians, and strongly opposed to their exploitation. [24] As would be expected, then, he was often very critical of any excessive use of corporal punishment in the missions:

> *I have no doubt that with regard to the punishment we are discussing, there probably have been some irregularities and excesses on the part of some Padres. We all run this risk. [...T]he trust [the native Californians] have in us is based on the fact that when we came here, none of them were Christians. And we have given them birth in Christ. We have all come here and remained here for the sole purpose of their well-being and salvation. And I believe everyone realizes we love them.* [25]

That the conversion and education of the Indians was Serra's main purpose is made crystal clear by his reaction to a December 13, 1775 attack on the Mission San Diego de Alcalá. A large group of Kumeyaay Indians, coming from some neighboring villages, had destroyed the mission, killing one of the friars and wounding another. Serra wrote to the viceroy of New Spain:

> *The Padre has been killed, the mission has been burned down, and its many, beautiful ornaments, sacred vessels, images, and baptismal, marriage, and burial records have been destroyed [...]. Señor Excelentísimo: One of the most important things I requested [...] at the beginning of these conquests was that, if the Indians were to kill me, whether they be gentiles or Christians, they should be forgiven. [...L]et the murderer live so he can be saved, which is the purpose of our coming here and the reason for forgiving him. Help him to understand, with some moderate punishment, that he is being pardoned in accordance with our law, which orders us to forgive offenses and to prepare him, not for his death, but for eternal life.* [26]

Serra died in 1784, in the mission of San Carlos Borromeo de Carmelo. His holiness and his love of God and neighbor were immediately recognized by those whom he had served. His fellow friar Francisco Palóu, who had accompanied him to Alta California, wrote:

> *As soon as the bells were rung, the entire pueblo gathered together and wept for the death of their beloved Padre, who had given them birth in the Lord. They loved him more than if he had been their natural father. They all wanted to see him in order to ease the sorrow that had taken hold of their hearts and be able to express it with tears. The throng of people, Indians as well as soldiers and sailors, was so large that it was necessary to close the door to be able to place Su Paternidad in the coffin [...]. The body remained in his cell until nightfall. A steady stream of people went in and out of the cell, praying to him and touching his venerable hands and face with rosaries and medals. Without mincing words they would call him "Padre Santo," "Padre Bendito," and other affectionate names that stemmed from the love they felt for him and from the heroic virtues they had seen in him during his life.* [27]

Serra was not a perfect man, and many testimonies of the brothers describe his difficult character. Yet, despite his mistakes, he never held back in any way, instead allowing his life to be consumed by the desire to communicate Jesus Christ to all those whom he encountered. His motto reminds us of his tireless passion: *Siempre adelante!* Ever forward!

III.
DAMIEN DE VEUSTER

We now move further west to the Hawaiian Islands, and forward a century.

HAWAI'I

Statue of Damien de Veuster, National Statuary Hall, Washington, D.C.

When Hawaii became the fiftieth state of the United States of America, it donated statues of two influential people to the National Statuary Hall of the Capitol in Washington, D.C. One was a statue of Kamehameha I, also known as Kamehameha the Great (c. 1736-1819), the first king of the united Hawaiian Islands. The other statue – selected by almost unanimous acclaim – was that of a Flemish Catholic missionary who had spent his life on the island of Molokai taking care of lepers, and who himself died of leprosy in 1889. That man was Damien de Veuster.

Damien was born in 1840 a few miles from Leuven, to a family of farmers. As a teenager, he was deeply moved when he heard a missionary preach, and immediately asked to be admitted to the Congregation of the Sacred Hearts of Jesus and Mary, a religious order born in France in the 1800s, during a period of missionary fervor within both the Protestant and Catholic churches.

During his novitiate, a desire to leave for faraway missions grew in Damien, and he would often pray for this desire's fulfillment before the statue of St. Francis Xavier.

When his brother Pamphile, who was also a member of the Congregation, was forced to give up his mission to the Hawaiian Islands due to illness, Damien wrote a letter to the Superior General asking to be sent in his place, thus bypassing the rector who did not think him suitable for the task. In October 1863, he set off from the port of Bremen on a five-month long trip to Honolulu. In a letter to Pamphile, he wrote:

My dear brother, [...] I am sorry I am neither a poet nor a writer, to send you a good description of my new country, so I shall content myself with saying a few words about it. Our archipelago lies on the border of the tropics, between twenty-one and twenty-three degrees north from the equator. For two months, June and July, we have the sun directly over our heads; still the heat is not so great as I thought. The climate is delightful, so that strangers easily become accustomed to it, and generally enjoy better health here than in their own country. The archipelago is made up of eight islands, four of which are large and four small. Hawaii, the one on which I am stationed, is larger than all the others together. It is as large as Belgium, if not larger. In the centre are three volcanoes, two of which appear to be extinct. The third is still active, and it is in its neighbourhood that Providence has destined me to be placed. From one end of my district to the other you have to walk on lava, that is, the stone and iron that the immense heat of the volcano has melted at different times and caused to flow towards the sea. [28]

[...] It is impossible to express how immensely happy a missionary is when he sees the new land that he must water with his sweat to gain uncivilized souls for God. [29]

Damien was ordained a priest in Honolulu at the age of 24.

My dear brother: On Ember Saturday in the week of Pentecost we were ordained priests, and the next day said our first Masses in the Cathedral of Honolulu. Recall the feelings you yourself experienced, the day you had the happiness to stand at the altar for the first time to offer the Divine Victim of our salvation. Mine were the same with this difference, that you were surrounded by friends and brothers in religion, while I was surrounded by children, recent converts, who had come from all parts to see their new spiritual Fathers, whose arrival they had so long desired. [30]

Damien after his ordination

During his first nine years as a missionary (1864-1873), Damien worked on the island of Hawaii. He built churches, learned the local language, and developed a particular affection for the native *Kanakas*, and their food and customs. The Catholic community continued to grow, and Damien was cherished by the Kanakas, who called him *Kamiano* because they could not pronounce the 'D' in 'Damien.' His superiors, on the other hand, were often very critical of his impulsive nature, his sudden decisions, and his somewhat difficult temperament.

During that time, the Kingdom of Hawaii was struck by an epidemic of leprosy that forced the king to quarantine the infected people to the northern part of the island of Molokai, one of the smallest islands of the Hawaiian archipelago. The conditions in the leper colony quickly became serious. People for whom there was no hope were abandoned there with the bare minimum needed for survival and without anyone to care for them.

In 1873, the Honolulu bilingual newspaper *Nuhou* published an article about the leper colony on the island of Molokai, suggesting some ways to help, and launching the following appeal:

> *And if a noble Christian priest, pastor or sister should be inspired to go and sacrifice a life to console these poor wretches, that would be a royal soul to shine forever on a throne reared by human love.* [31]

Damien volunteered to go and left for Kalaupapa, the place on the island of Molokai where the lepers were confined. In a letter to his brother Pamphile, he wrote:

> *My dear Brother, God has deigned to choose your unworthy brother to assist the poor people attacked by that terrible malady, so often mentioned in the Gospel: leprosy. For the last ten years this plague has been spreading in the islands, and at last the Government felt itself obliged to isolate those affected with it. Shut up in a corner of the*

island of Molokai, between inaccessible cliffs and the sea, these unfortunate creatures are condemned to perpetual exile. Out of two thousand in all who have been sent here, some eight hundred are still living, and among them a certain number of Catholics. A priest was wanted; but here was a difficulty. For, as all communication was forbidden with the rest of the islands, a priest who should be placed here must consider himself shut up with the lepers for the rest of his life; and [our superior] declared that he would not impose this sacrifice on any of us. So, [...] I offered myself [...]. Consequently, on the 11th of last May, a steamer landed me here, together with a batch of fifty lepers, whom the authorities had collected in the island of Hawaii. [32]

Damien's first impact with the reality of Molokai terrified him. The despair of those who know that they are destined to die had led the lepers to live lives of desperate dissolution. Women were forced into prostitution, orphaned children were abandoned to the violence of adults, and the sick were left to their own devices without anyone to care for them. There were no doctors or nurses, and often the dead were left unburied. In short, Damien confronted an environment utterly lacking in human dignity.

Leprosy, as far as is known, is incurable: it seems to begin by a corruption of the blood. Discoloured patches appear on the skin, especially on the cheeks; and the parts affected lose their feeling. After a time, this discoloration covers the whole body; then ulcers begin to open, chiefly at the extremities. The flesh is eaten away, and gives out a fetid odour;

Damien in Molokai,
© Archivio Storico della Congregazione dei
Sacri Cuori di Gesù e di Maria, Roma.

even the breath of the leper becomes so foul that the air around is poisoned with it. I have had great difficulty in getting accustomed to such an atmosphere. One day, at the Sunday Mass, I found myself so stifled that I thought I must leave the altar to breathe a little of the outer air, but I restrained myself, thinking of our Lord when He commanded them to open the grave of Lazarus, notwithstanding Martha's words, "by now there will be a stench." Now my sense of smell does not cause me so much inconvenience, and I enter the huts of the lepers without difficulty. Sometimes, indeed, I still feel some repugnance when I have to hear the confessions of those near their end, whose wounds are full of maggots. Often, also, I scarce know how to administer Extreme Unction, when both hands and feet are nothing but raw wounds. [33]

Overcoming his initial disgust, Damien began to live with the lepers, understanding that he simply could not follow the orders given to him by his superiors: "Don't touch them, don't let them touch you, and don't eat with them." Though he saw the need to be prudent, Damien wanted to be with the lepers. He began smoking a pipe because the smell of tobacco covered the stench, and he constantly sought new ways to communicate with the lepers.

Damien with a group of lepers in Molokai
© *Archivio Storico della Congregazione dei Sacri Cuori di Gesù e di Maria, Roma.*

As for me, I make myself a leper with the lepers, to gain all for Jesus Christ. That is why in preaching, I say, We lepers, not, My brethren, as in Europe. [34]

During his fifteen years on Molokai, "the island of death," Damien gave himself completely to the mission. He cured ulcers, built houses, and dug graves. In fifteen years he built more than one thousand coffins. Under his leadership, the community established laws to govern their common life, built huts and larger houses, founded schools, created factories, and built chapels, refectories, and dormitories where everyone was welcome, Catholic and non-Catholic alike.

A lack of hope had caused the lepers to lose all sense of their own dignity. Damien realized that work gave back to these sick people an understanding of their own value. The orphans were also one of his priorities. Damien built two orphanages because he saw that when parents died, dozens of children remained without protection. He suffered greatly whenever one of his little orphans died.

Damien with a group of children in Molokai
© *Archivio Storico della Congregazione dei Sacri Cuori di Gesù e di Maria, Roma.*

He renovated the dilapidated church dedicated to St. Philomena, and it became a reference point for the Catholic community. Attentive care for the liturgy and for music, especially singing, provided the people with the means to express their value as human beings, aware of themselves as children of God. Damien was able to foster this sense of dignity among the lepers because he recognized that his strength was rooted in the Eucharist.

The Church of St. Philomena
© Archivio Storico della
Congregazione dei Sacri Cuori
di Gesù e di Maria, Roma.

[…] I always have our Lord in the Tabernacle. In fact, without the Blessed Sacrament a position like mine would not be tolerable. But having our Lord with me, I am always happy, and work cheerfully for the relief of the unfortunate lepers. [35]

Because of the possibility of contagion, Damien could neither leave the island nor receive visits. One time, because the bishop was forbidden from docking at the island, Damien went out to him in a small boat and confessed from a distance, speaking in French.

Damien's "We lepers" soon became reality. In December 1884, while soaking his feet in a tub of hot water, he realized that he could not feel the heat, which he immediately recognized as a symptom of leprosy. Despite his illness, he continued to work with his usual stubbornness, as well as a healthy sense of irony. He decided that he wanted to be buried by the tree where he had spent his first night on Molokai when he was still terrorized by the death that surrounded him. But the deaths on Molokai were so numerous that room for graves was becoming scarce:

Damien after contracting leprosy
© Archivio Storico della
Congregazione dei Sacri Cuori di
Gesù e di Maria, Roma.

I was quite vexed the other day to find they had begun to dig a grave just by the large cross, in the very spot which I had so long reserved for myself! I had to insist on the place being left vacant. [36]

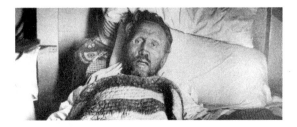

Damien on his deathbed
© Archivio Storico della
Congregazione dei Sacri Cuori di
Gesù e di Maria, Roma.

It was there that he was buried after death took him peacefully in 1889, at the age of 48. On his grave, which is now in Belgium, there is a sentence that he wrote to his family: "My greatest happiness is to serve the Lord in His poor and ill children, the leftovers of society."

Through his simple life Damien gave a witness of charity that struck many men and women, even those far from the Catholic world, as we shall see at the end of this journey.

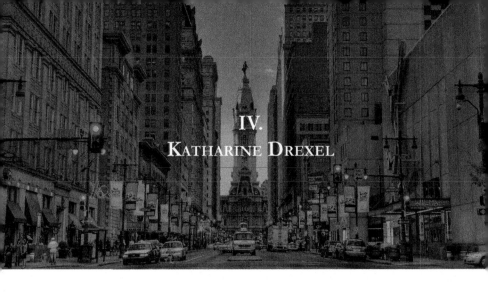

IV.
KATHARINE DREXEL

The final leg of our journey takes us to Philadelphia, between the end of the nineteenth century and the beginning of the twentieth. There we find Katharine Drexel, a great educator and founder of schools for Native and African Americans. Ahead of her time, Katharine Drexel ministered to these minority populations by meeting their material, spiritual, and educational needs.

Drexel lived during a turbulent time in United States history. The Civil War had been the culmination of the conflict between the North and the South with regard to slavery, but institutional, legal discrimination ensured that racism remained profoundly rooted within American society. This same period saw comprehensive attempts to resolve the so-called "Indian Problem." In 1870, United States president Ulysses S. Grant implemented the "Peace Policy," with the intention of gathering all Native Americans within reservations. It was due to this policy that many Native Americans were compelled by force to re-establish themselves in territories in the

western United States. This process of displacement had the obvious consequence of increasing tensions between Native Americans and whites. The Native Americans had access to schooling, but the ultimate aim of this education was a sort of forced integration, with the goal of eliminating the traditions and customs of the Native Americans. One of the main slogans of the time was: "Kill the Indian, and Save the Man." Native Americans obtained the right to become citizens only in 1924.

The human adventure of Katharine Drexel, her work, and her mission, are closely intertwined with these historical events. Katharine was born in 1858 in Philadelphia, to one of the richest and most influential families in the United States. Her grandfather, Francis Martin Drexel (1792-1863), perfectly embodied the American Dream: a portrait painter who emigrated from Austria, he became after a few years a successful banker. His son, Katharine's father, Francis Anthony Drexel, followed in his footsteps, and gained international stature in the world of high finance.

Her family's wealth allowed Katharine a privileged childhood, full of rare experiences and travels in America and abroad, and provided her with a rigorous education. The family was profoundly religious and famous in the city for acts of charity toward the poor. Upon the death of Katherine's mother, it was discovered that she had regularly paid the rent for 150 families. From her youthful diaries we can glean that Katharine was a well-educated girl with a deep religiosity:

A young Katharine Drexel
© Sisters of the Blessed Sacrament Archive, Bensalem, PA

> *I resolve that during the next year: I shall try to overcome impurity, pride, and vanity; to speak French; to pay attention to prayers and to studies; to read a life of a saint [...]; to try to go to confession less as if I were going to an execution; and during the day to offer up all my actions to God every time the clock strikes.* [37]

Katherine was educated in the faith through a constant dialogue that she established with her spiritual father, James O'Connor, her pastor in Philadelphia who eventually became bishop of Omaha, Nebraska. She would turn to him often, especially when, having turned twenty years old, she began to question herself with urgency about her definitive vocation, often in a dramatic and even sometimes melancholy tone:

To the extent that I can read my own heart, I am not happy. I have a void within that only God could fill. [...] Now, the question about my own state of life resolves itself, I think, in this: What can I do for God's greater glory and service? To tell the truth, it appears to me that God calls me to the religious life [...] Please tell me, dear Father, what should I do to save my own soul, to save as many souls as possible, to devote myself and all that I have to God and to His Church? Everything, everything, everything (there is no exception) ends and will end [...]. The only important question, whose solution determines how one's life has been spent, is the state of my soul at the moment of death. Infinite unhappiness or infinite happiness! There is no middle path, it's one or the other. [38]

Katharine felt increasingly that she was being called to dedicate herself completely to God, in a life of contemplation and prayer; yet in these same years she became interested in the dramatic situation of the Native Americans, above all through the accounts she received from O'Connor, who in his letters described their condition in Nebraska. Katharine strongly desired to help them in their material and spiritual needs. And a trip through the South and exposure to the narratives of missionaries had sparked an interest in addressing the living conditions of African Americans.

With these desires and this question of vocation in her heart, at twenty-eight years of age Katharine departed with her sisters on a long voyage through Europe. In Rome, she had the opportunity to meet in private audience with Pope Leo XIII. A few decades later she would describe this encounter in the following way:

Kneeling at his feet, my girlish fancy thought that surely God's Vicar would not refuse me. So I pleaded for missionary priests for Bishop O'Connor's Indians. To my astonishment His Holiness responded, "Why not, my child, yourself become a missionary?" [39]

Katharine asked herself: Could the pope's question be a sign? Was it truly a call to become a missionary? What should she do with her desire for contemplation and prayer? The invitation from the pope left her restless and sad for the duration of her return sea voyage. Back in America, Katharine visited the missions of South

Dakota, together with Bishop O'Connor, and began to donate a great deal of time and money to support the construction of schools and churches for the Native Americans.

> *[Dear Bishop O'Connor], several times during our trip out West, I remember you said to me with an amused expression, "What makes you look so sad?" My heart indeed was sad, is sad, because in your judgement I am condemned to living in a world whose ways I detest. I cannot say, 'My God and my All' as long as I am not consecrated to Our Lord. As He is, or as I desire Him truly to be 'my All,' I wish to love Him in poverty, chastity, and obedience.* [40]

Five years would pass before Katharine, continually in dialogue with O'Connor, came to understand that she was being called to found a new religious order for aid and mission to the Native and African Americans: the Sisters of the Blessed Sacrament for Indians and Colored People, whose missionary activity would begin in 1894.

Sisters of the Blessed Sacrament for Indians and Colored People, 1894

The name was inspired by Katharine's conviction that the source of all action comes from Christ: all her courageous and audacious acts were born out of a love for the Eucharist. At the same time, she was convinced that the Christ of the Eucharist was found in the faces of those around her:

> *Find Jesus in the representatives of Himself, the children He has placed under your care, find Him in the grown-up dusky creatures who will come to your door at Christmas; find Him in the hearts of your Sisters and in the hearts of those children whom you have been instrumental in bringing to Baptism and the Holy Table. Thus Jesus will be praised and served by you everywhere and in all.* [41]

During Katharine's long life, the Sisters of the Blessed Sacrament opened more than 50 missions, with schools, churches, colleges, and centers of professional formation, for Native and African Americans throughout many parts of the United States.

Missions and schools founded by
Katharine Drexel

The life of the sisters teemed with work, but also included moments of silence and prayer. Katharine dedicated herself tirelessly to the various works of the order, personally dealing with architects, lawyers, and local and ecclesiastical authorities. Despite being called "the Millionaire Nun" or "The Richest Sister in the World," Katharine lived a very simple life, dedicated to the poor.

In 1902, Drexel opened the first Catholic school for the Navajo people in Arizona.

St. Michael Indian School, Arizona, 1902

The population of the Navajos had been decimated during the deportations, and those who remained were abandoned to their own devices in the desert. Many Indian leaders were suspicious of dealing with whites. Despite difficulties in fully understanding the traditions of the natives, and the ever-present risk of a paternalistic approach towards caring for them, Katharine's work was exceptional in those years. Her approach to educating Native Americans was diametrically opposed to the "Kill the Indian, save the man" ideology. Katharine overcame suspicion and resistance: she met with tribal elders and established a friendly relationship with the native populations, developing educational programs that, rather than neglecting or destroying their cultural roots, tried to engage and further develop them.

Katharine Drexel with the Navajos
© *Sisters of the Blessed Sacrament Archive, Bensalem, PA*

[We will found] five missions, I think, before July. One of the missions is for the Navajos, who number about 22,000; the Navajos are a nation of farmers and shepherds and with the wool of their sheep they make blankets that are sold at $150 each. I thought that for them an industrial school [would be a good idea], where you can teach agriculture, shoemaking, and metallurgy. [42]

To the traditional school curriculum were added professional classes that allowed students to learn manual labor. Such an approach was not common at that time. She also hired as a teacher a Navajo weaver, to teach the young students how to weave blankets.

Often Katharine participated in the traditional celebrations of the Navajos and, in her desire to empathize with them, even tried peyote, a hallucinogen used in certain rites. She remarked that the ceremony had similarities to the celebration of the Eucharist, but found the peyote taste particularly bitter.

Visiting the Navajos in Arizona, 1927
© *Sisters of the Blessed Sacrament Archive, Bensalem, PA*

In the South, Katharine Drexel founded missions and schools for African Americans. Here it was mainly the hostility of whites, even within the Catholic Church, that hindered the work of the sisters. It was hard to find priests willing to work with her. After local residents of Nashville, Tennessee had tried in every way to keep the nuns from opening a school for African Americans, Katharine wrote to her sisters, inviting them to be "shrewd as serpents and simple as doves," and joking that that they would not find a good accommodation there, much like Jesus couldn't find one in Bethlehem.

A school for African-American children
© Sisters of the Blessed Sacrament Archive, Bensalem, PA

Sometimes it is fitting that we find no place for us or for our work. The Cave of Bethlehem was once the great teacher of the World! We must never neglect to think of Him with whom we are proud to be in love! We must also be enamored of His humiliation! [43]

Katharine Drexel with African-American children, Port Arthur, TX
© Sisters of the Blessed Sacrament Archive, Bensalem, PA

In Beaumont, Texas, the nuns of the Blessed Sacrament were opposed by the Ku Klux Klan, the racist secret society founded after the Civil War. The Klan targeted the school and the church, and intimidating phrases threatening blacks were posted on its walls: if the sisters continued their work in the mission, they warned, the Klan would use dynamite to destroy it. Adding to the danger, the mission could not count on the protection of the authorities, who were often themselves Klan members. The situation quickly became very tense: Katharine procured bodyguards for the priests and the property, and entrusted the nuns to God in prayer. Providentially, on March 25, 1922, the local headquarters of the Ku Klux Klan was destroyed by a tornado, and since then the school and the church founded by Katharine have never been threatened again.

Perhaps Katharine's most significant contribution to the education of African-Americans was the founding of Xavier University in New Orleans, in 1915. In order to be able to teach, the sisters of the Blessed Sacrament returned to school at the Catholic University of America, and Katharine herself went back to school at the age of sixty-two. Xavier University – which today has about 3,000 students – guaranteed access to higher education for people of color for the first time in American history, anticipating U.S. legislation by about fifty years. The sisters's inclusive educational ideal was expressed on a plaque placed at the entrance of the University: "God's greatest work on earth is man; man's master art is leading men to God."

In 1935, while in St. Louis, Katharine suffered a stroke that forced her into a state of almost total immobility for the last twenty years of her life. At age seventy-six, she resigned from the office of Superior General of the order and retired to its headquarters, where she spent her days living a life of contemplation and prayer – that life which she had so desired as a young woman. Finally, she said, she had learned how to pray.

The extraordinary life of Katharine Drexel was guided by the certainty that God fulfills the desires that He puts in one's heart. As she wrote after visiting the sisters engaged in a work for the Navajos:

Do you know it seemed like the realization of years, yes, longings of the last fifteen years? When I looked at you, the virgin mothers of the poor Navajos, my heart was full of gratitude to God because He had beyond all expectations, fulfilled the desire He Himself had given me, to do something for these poor pagans. [...] And so, on this visit I looked up in wonder at God's wonderful ways and thought how little we imagine what may be the result of listening and acting on a desire He puts into the heart. If He puts it into the heart He will bless it, if we try to act upon it, and great will be the effect before God. [44]

V.

THE FRUITS OF THE MISSION

What traces were left by the often discrete witnesses of these saints? How did these people speak to the whole world from their little corner of the earth? What does it mean, to use a phrase from Pope Benedict XVI, that "Even when they are few in number, saints change the world, and great saints remain as forces for change throughout history"? [45] One characteristic of Christian witness is the capacity to transcend space and time. But what does such transcendence look like in the cases of our American saints?

1. The *How* of a Saint's Witness: "Passing the Baton"

Saints change the world because they are never isolated, and their witness lives and continues to work within the story of a people, the Church, that manifests a sort of "passing of the baton." The martyrdom of the North American Jesuits, for example, has produced unexpected fruits, and their story proves true the old adage of Tertullian, who said: "The blood of the martyrs is the seed of the Church."

After a long period of time marked by war and the persecution of missionaries, the Iroquois opted for peace, and many of them converted to Christianity. The martyrdom of the North American Jesuits at the hands of the Iroquois began to bring forth unexpected fruits. Thirty years after their death, an eighteen-year-old Mohawk woman named Kateri Tekakwitha (1656-1680) converted to Christianity and began living a life of total dedication to Christ.

Portrait of Kateri Tekakwitha, (c. 1690), by Fr. Chauchetière

Together with a friend, and fighting against prejudice from her tribe, she founded a group of young women who gave themselves to Christ in virginity. At the age of 24 she died of the smallpox that she had contracted in her youth. Kateri, who had become known as the "Lily of the Mohawks," was one of the most unexpected products of the Jesuit missions in New France during the seventeenth century. The fruits of the martyrdom of Brébeuf and his companions did not stop here but continued into the following centuries. At the beginning of the nineteenth century many Iroquois from an area around Montréal entered the service of some fur trappers who were working in the Rocky Mountains. After a trade crisis some of the Iroquois people decided to remain in the West, especially in Oregon, and became hunters and guides. A group of twenty-four Christian Iroquois joined the local Salish (Flathead) tribe and told them about the Jesuit missionaries they had met in Québec, thus introducing Christianity into this part of North America. The Flatheads sent a number of delegations to St. Louis insisting that Jesuit missionaries be sent to them. In this way, Christian communities were formed among the Indians of these areas. At the end of the nineteenth century, these communities were revitalized thanks to Katherine Drexel, who was well acquainted with the story of Kateri Tekakwitha and had visited her grave. At the same time, in Europe, the letters of Brébeuf, Garnier, Jogues, and companions – those same letters that we read in the first section of our journey – were widely circulated. The letters reached many Jesuit houses where for the next three centuries thousands of young men asked to be sent as missionaries to the New World.

The successes and failures of these men, and the long chain of encounters that slowly, over two centuries, almost by contagion,[46] propagated Christianity among the Native Americans from the Great Lakes to the Pacific Northwest, cannot but bring to mind the words of Jean de Brébeuf: "never will this field produce fruit except through mildness and patience." [47]

2. The *What* of the Saint's Witness: "I am Christ's"

Saints change the world, but not because they are heroes. A hero's witness ends with his or her death, or it continues only as a memory of somebody great, but gone. What, instead, do saints witness to with their lives? While they provided food, care, assistance, and education, the saints also offered what is most precious: Christ Himself.

A newspaper article relates the following story:

In 2002, then-Archbishop of New York Cardinal Edward Egan visited an elementary school in St. Mark's Parish in Harlem, a very poor African American neighborhood. In a hall crowded with parents and relatives, after the children's pageant, Egan struggled to reach the exit. Amid the crowd that thronged to greet him was an old African American man gasping for air, in a wheelchair. He reached out, and when he managed to reach the Cardinal, he pulled him close. He whispered into the Cardinal's ear with the little strength he had left: "Mother Katharine Drexel paid for my piano lessons!" Egan, barely understanding what the man was saying, managed to exclaim: "How nice of Mother Katharine Drexel!" and then: "And you, sir, what is your name?" "My name is Lionel Hampton," the old man responded. The Cardinal was floored. Lionel Hampton was a legend, one of the greatest names in the history of jazz. And here was the man, sitting before him in a wheelchair at the age of ninety-four. Hampton would die a few months later. The educational genius of Katharine Drexel not only understood and nurtured the talent of a poor black boy, but she also taught him something. Today, Lionel Hampton is remembered not only for his amazing music, but also for the hundreds of houses he built for poor families in New York. [48]

33

The witness of the saints is not concentrated in their heroism, or their personality, but in the source of their joy: "I am Christ's." Their strength comes from its transparency: saints give a glimpse of what is working within them. This is why one's temperament is never an impediment to holiness: the best defense against this idea comes from the most unlikely sources. The story of Damien de Veuster, the Leper Saint of Hawaii, resonates in this regard. His fame, celebrated by many, also provoked some polemics. Shortly after his death, Charles McEwen Hyde, a Presbyterian missionary in Honolulu, described Damien as coarse, dirty, and stubborn, and therefore not saintly. A letter he wrote was published in various newspapers and was widely circulated. The writer Robert Louis Stevenson, an agnostic son of a Presbyterian, wrote an open letter to Hyde in Fr. Damien's defense, which he ended up publishing at his own expense because he could not find a publisher. Although the author of *Treasure Island* never personally met Fr. Damien, he visited Hawaii soon after the missionary's death. What he saw and the stories he gathered struck him profoundly.

Charles McEwen Hyde   *Robert Louis Stevenson*

> *When I visited the lazaretto Damien was already in his resting grave. But such information as I have, I gathered on the spot in conversation with those who knew him well and long: some indeed who revered his memory; but others who had sparred and wrangled with him, who beheld him with no halo, who perhaps regarded him with small respect, and through whose unprepared and scarcely partial communications the plain, human features of the man shone on me convincingly. [...] Had you [visited Molokai...] you would have understood that life in the lazaretto is an ordeal from which the nerves of a man's spirit shrink [...].*
>
> *It is not the fear of possible infection. That seems a little thing when compared with the pain, the pity, and the disgust of the visitor's surroundings, and the atmosphere of affliction, disease, and physical disgrace in which he breathes. [...] It was a different place when Damien came there, and made his great renunciation, and slept that first night under a tree amidst his rotting brethren: alone with pestilence; and looking forward (with what courage, with what pitiful sinkings of dread, God only knows) to a lifetime of dressing sores and stumps.* [49]

Stevenson rejected the idealized image of the missionary that was in circulation. On the contrary it was Fr. Damien's humanity, with all of its limits, that struck him. In his weakness, the man who was called "coarse, dirty, and stubborn" became all the more fascinating.

There are many (not Catholics merely) who require their heroes and saints to be infallible; to these the story will always be painful; not to the true lovers, patrons, and servants of mankind. [...]. [You said that] Damien was coarse. It is very possible. You make us sorry for the lepers who had only a coarse old peasant for their friend and father. But you, who were so refined, why were you not there to cheer them with the lights of culture? Or may I remind you that we have some reason to doubt if John the Baptist were genteel; and in the case of Peter, on whose career you doubtless dwell approvingly in the pulpit, no doubt at all that he was a "coarse, headstrong" fisherman! Yet, even in our Protestant Bibles Peter is called Saint.

[...] You had a father: suppose this [derogatory] tale were about him, and some informant brought it to you, proof in hand: [...] I suppose you would regret the circumstance? [...] Well, the man who tried to do what Damien did, is my father, and the father of the man [you meet in a] bar, and the father of all who love goodness; and he was your father too, if God had given you grace to see it. [50]

Despite the many disagreements between the Catholic and Protestant missionaries that were so common during the time in which Damien lived, there were examples of ecumenism *avant la lettre*, and today Damien, a Catholic saint, is also venerated in the Episcopal Church of the United States of America.

Finally, consider an episode that shows the spread of Damien's story beyond all cultural and religious borders. Mahatma Gandhi was aware of the story of Damien and cited it as one of his sources of inspiration:

The political and journalistic world can boast of very few heroes who compare with Fr. Damien of Molokai. The Catholic Church, on the contrary, counts by the thousands those who after the example of Fr. Damien have devoted themselves to the victims of leprosy. It is worthwhile to look for the sources of such heroism. [51]

Gandhi recognized that what is most interesting about the saints is not their heroism but the source of their exceptional lives.

3. The *When* of the Saint's Witness: an Encounter with Us

While talking about the American saints is edifying, a greater benefit comes from entering into a dialogue with them.

The chain of encounters that led the stories of these American saints through time and space has now reached the present. In the past few months, in the course of preparing this exhibit, we have met men and women whose lives were changed by encounters with these saints. Rubén Mendoza, an archaeologist from California of Native American and Mexican descent, was initially opposed to the Catholic missionaries of Mexico and California. Holding to the dream of a pure indigenous past, he saw the missionaries as invading destroyers of indigenous peoples and cultures, until he discovered through encounters with Franciscan friars and work excavating some of the missions the humanity of Junípero Serra, and thus came to embrace Serra's role in his mixed heritage. Audrey Taguchi, an eighty-year-old woman from Honolulu, told us about how she was healed of an incurable tumor through the intercession of Damien de Veuster. Joy Vostatek explained to us that her family was saved by the educational genius of Katharine Drexel. We went to Kanawake, an Indian reserve near Montréal, and saw that still today the Mohawk people gather around the tomb of Kateri Tekakwitha. The witness of these saints and the fullness of life that shines through their faces have made them our companions, just as the Church has suggested by canonizing them in recent years.

Indeed, although our circumstances are very different from those of the seventeenth century, the Jesuit martyrs continue to show us what it means to be unashamed of Christ in a world that so often denies Him, and what it means to live with a certainty that no one can take away. Martyrdom can be giving one's life, as so many Christians are being asked to do today, or the simplicity of daily witnessing to Him. During the canonization of Kateri Tekakwitha in 2012, Benedict XVI indicated her simple life as a help for us "to live where we are, loving Jesus without denying who we are"! [52]

Junípero Serra's tireless missionary drive shows us how the desire to communicate Jesus is necessary if those who have encountered Jesus do not want their hearts to wither. Pope Francis, who canonized Serra in 2015, cited him as "the embodiment of a Church which goes forth":

> [...] a Church which goes forth, a Church which sets out to bring everywhere the reconciling tenderness of God. [...] Father Serra had a motto [...] which shaped the way he lived: siempre adelante! Keep moving forward! For him, this was the way to continue experiencing the joy of the Gospel, to keep his heart from growing numb, from being anesthetized. He kept moving forward, because the Lord was waiting. He kept going, because his brothers and sisters were waiting. He kept going forward to the end of his life. Today, like him, may we be able to say: Forward! Let's keep moving forward! [53]

Damien's boundless love, able to reach and move people in every age and from every background, forces us, as Benedict XVI suggested at Damien's canonization in 2009, to ask who "our" lepers are, "to open our eyes to the forms of leprosy that disfigure the humanity of our brethren and still today call for the charity of our presence as servants, beyond that of our generosity." [54]

Finally, Katharine Drexel's faithfulness to the desires of her own heart, even when they were uncomfortable, and Leo XIII's question to her, What are you going to do?, show us that Christianity continues to happen like it did in the beginning, precisely when someone asks, "And what about you?" During his visit to the United States in 2015, Pope Francis asked the same question.

When she spoke to Pope Leo XIII of the needs of the missions, the Pope [...] asked her pointedly: "What about you? What are you going to do?". Those words changed Katharine's life, because they reminded her that, in the end, every Christian man and woman, by virtue of baptism, has received a mission. [...] "What about you?" I encourage you to be renewed in the joy and wonder of that first encounter with Jesus, and to draw from that joy renewed fidelity and strength. [55]

Here, on this point of renewed joy found in meeting Jesus, we conclude our journey with the American saints. Missionaries, adventurers, authors of gestures of extreme charity, founders of schools, educators: "our" saints were not perfect, and their attempts to embrace those they met and communicate the joy of the Gospel sometimes included disappointments and failures. But in the ongoing struggle to change themselves and pursue personal conversion, which predominates in their writings, the desire to know and love Christ emerges with great clarity. Their extraordinary lives have not led us to measure the disproportion between "us" and "them"; instead, they inflame our desire to be evermore "attached to Jesus."

EPILOGUE
OUR LADY OF GOOD HELP

Nicholas Erickson © 2016

The stories told in this booklet show how, in an unexpected way, "the saints changed the world": even when it seemed like their lives and their witnesses did not yield immediate fruit, time revealed their fecundity. At the end of this journey through their stories and writings, Pope Benedict's affirmation that the saints "continue to be the transformational force in every time period" rings ever more true.

We conclude our journey with a final story, which takes place in American territory and which has slowly, silently, traversed the decades: the events of a Marian apparition which took place in Wisconsin during the middle of the nineteenth century. Though forgotten for decades, the apparition was recently recognized and approved by the Bishop of Green Bay.

***

The Shrine of Our Lady of Good Help is located in Champion, a few miles from the city of Green Bay, in northern Wisconsin.

Champion, near
Green Bay, Wisconsin

The story of the apparitions, which occurred in 1859, begins far from Wisconsin, in the village of Dion le Val, twenty-five miles from Brussels, where on January 30, 1831, Maria Adèle Joseph Brise was born.[56] During her adolescent years Adèle, who received a fervent education in the faith and developed a special devotion to the Virgin Mary, confided to her spiritual director that she would like one day to become a missionary.[57] In 1855, Adèle emigrated together with her family to the United States; at that time, this was the special goal and privilege of anyone who was in search of stability and prosperity. They headed to northern Wisconsin, then a frontier territory, to a place called Bay Settlement, close to present-day Green Bay, where a small Belgian community already existed.

One day, towards the beginning of October, 1859, around a year and a half after the much more famous apparitions in Lourdes, Adèle was walking through the countryside when she saw, through two trees, a woman dressed in white, with a yellow band around her waist and a crown of stars around her head, characteristics quite similar to those found in other Marian apparitions. A few years later, Adèle's friend and confidante, Sister Pauline LaPlante, transcribed the story of the apparitions:

She [Adele] was going to the grist mill about four miles from here [Champion] with a sack of wheat on her head [...]. As Adele came near the place, she saw a lady all in white standing between two trees, one a maple, the other a hemlock. Adele was frightened and stood still. The vision slowly disappeared, leaving a white cloud after it. Adele continued on her errand and returned home without seeing anything more. She told her parents what had happened, and they wondered what it could be — maybe a poor soul who needed prayers?

On the following Sunday, she had to pass here again on her way to Mass at Bay Settlement, about eleven miles from her home[...]. This time, she was not alone, but was accompanied by her sister Isabel and a neighbor woman [Mrs. Vander Niessen]. When they came near the trees, the same lady in white was at the place where Adele had seen her before. Adele was again frightened and said, almost in a tone of reproach, "Oh, there is that lady again."

Adele had not the courage to go on. The other two did not see anything, but they could tell by Adele's look that she was afraid. They thought, too, that it might be a poor soul that needed prayers. They waited a few minutes, and Adele told them it was gone. It had disappeared as the first time, and all she could see was a little mist or white cloud. After Mass, Adele went to confession and told her confessor how she had been frightened at the sight of a lady in white. He [Father William Verhoef] bade her not to fear, and to speak to him of this outside of the confessional. Father Verhoef told her that if it were a heavenly messenger, she would see it again, and it would not harm her, but to ask in God's name who it was and what it desired of her. After that, Adele had more courage. She started home with her two companions, and a man who was clearing land for the Holy Cross Fathers at Bay Settlement accompanied them.

39

As they approached the hallowed spot, Adele could see the beautiful lady, clothed in dazzling white, with a yellow sash around her waist. Her dress fell to her feet in graceful folds. She had a crown of stars around her head, and her long, golden, wavy hair fell loosely around her shoulders. Such a heavenly light shone around her that Adele could hardly look back at her sweet face. Overcome by this heavenly light and the beauty of her amiable visitor, Adele fell on her knees.

"In God's name, who are you and what do you want of me?" asked Adele, as she had been directed.

"I am the Queen of Heaven, who prays for the conversion of sinners, and I wish you to do the same. You received Holy Communion this morning, and that is well. But you must do more. Make a general confession, and offer Communion for the conversion of sinners. If they do not convert and do penance, my Son will be obliged to punish them."

"Adele, who is it?" said one of the women. "O why can't we see her as you do" said another weeping.

"Kneel," said Adele, "the Lady says she is the Queen of Heaven." Our Blessed Lady turned, looked kindly at them, and said, **"Blessed are they that believe without seeing. What are you doing here in idleness...while your companions are working in the vineyard of my Son?"**

"What more can I do, dear Lady?" said Adele, weeping.

"Gather the children in this wild country and teach them what they should know for salvation."

"But how shall I teach them who know so little myself?" replied Adele.

"Teach them," replied her radiant visitor, "their catechism, how to sign themselves with the sign of the Cross, and how to approach the sacraments; that is what I wish you to do. Go and fear nothing. I will help you." [58]

News about the apparitions spread quickly and Adèle, responding to the Madonna's request, began to gather together children from throughout the countryside in order to teach them the catechism. Adèle's father built a small oratory near the site of the apparitions, and inside it he placed a small image of the Immaculate Heart of Mary donated by Fr. William Verhoef, Adèle's confessor. In 1861, the settlers of the area built a chapel which could hold up to a hundred people. On the entrance was written the phrase: "Notre Dame du Bon Secours, priez pour nous" [Our Lady of Good Help, pray for us], which gave the shrine its name. [59] Adèle began to raise funds for the construction of a school which could accommodate the youth of the area, and in 1868 the school opened its doors to about sixty students. In the meantime, in 1864 a group of third order Franciscans, under Adèle's guidance, had begun to live in community and to devote themselves to the care of the shrine and the school. These women were neither part of a religious order nor of a congregation: they remained secular members of the third order, adopting the simple habit, not taking any vows, and keeping their personal belongings, while being free to leave the community at any time. The only goal of the community was the education of the youth in the faith, according to the request that the Virgin had made of Adèle. Adèle's old desire – to consecrate herself to God and go on mission – had been fulfilled in an unexpected way.

In the following years, many miracles and healings were attributed to the intercession of the Madonna, but the event that sealed the story of this small shrine was "the Great Fire of Wisconsin." Also known as the Peshtigo Fire, after the place where it broke out, the great fire in October 1871 destroyed the Green Bay area, causing the deaths of more than two thousand people, and devastating an area of over three thousand square miles. The people who lived in the vicinity of the shrine gathered together to pray around the small chapel of Our Lady of Good Help, and the fire spared the small convent, the school, the chapel and the five acres consecrated to the Virgin. [60] It was thanks to this extraordinary event, attributed to the protection of the Madonna, that the shrine began to become well-known even outside of Wisconsin.

Adèle dedicated herself to the mission of education until her death, which came on July 5, 1896, and her work was continued by various religious orders which subsequently managed the school and the shrine; today it is the Fathers of Mercy who care for the shrine, while the school was definitively closed in 1968. [61]

In 2010, the apparitions obtained ecclesiastical approval from His Excellence David L. Ricken, Bishop of Green Bay, thus becoming the only Marian apparition officially recognized by the Church in the United States among the fifteen officially recognized apparitions worldwide.[62] The devotion to the shrine is still mostly local, though every year on August 15, numerous pilgrims from Wisconsin and other parts of the country gather together in the churchyard to celebrate mass with the bishop.

***

A noted Canadian philosopher has written: "Contemplation never crossed the ocean."[63] Perhaps he did not know about the centrality of contemplation in the lives of the American saints—both those who crossed the ocean, and those who were born in North America. As their stories show, nothing happened in their lives without contemplation, silence and prayer, without a constant rapport with Christ, the Author of all things. "Jesus is our true greatness," wrote Jean de Brébeuf to his companions. "Without the constant presence of our Divine Master in my poor little chapel," Damien observed, "I would have never been able to survive, but would have shared the same fate as that of the lepers of Molokai." Katharine Drexel asked her fellow sisters in a provocative manner: "Who has given you your strength? God! And He will give you even more strength this year."

The Madonna was mother and protector of the missions, model of purity for Kateri Tekakwitha, source of comfort and consolation for Jean de Brébeuf (before whom the Virgin appeared on several occasions), and a source of grit for Katharine Drexel, who was most faithful to her Rosary. Before leaving for Hawaii, Fr. Damien made a pilgrimage to the ancient Marian shrine of Our Lady of Montaigu, in Belgium, while Junípero Serra entrusted the fate of the settlers and the Indians to Our Lady of Guadalupe.

The shrine of Our Lady of Good Help, a hidden and discreet place in the heart of the North American continent, is a place where one can contemplate and pray on the very site where the Madonna chose to speak, encouraging the men and women of our own time to continue along the path first blazed by the American saints.

1 Charles Garnier, Letter to his brother, July 20, 1636, in François Roustang, S.J., ed., *Jesuit Missionaries to North America: Spiritual Writings and Biographical Sketches*, trans. Sr. M. Renelle, S.S.N.D. (San Francisco: Ignatius Press, 2006), 356.

2 From Jean de Brébeuf, "Instructions for the Fathers of Our Society Who Will be Sent to the Hurons," 1637, in Roustang, ed., *Jesuit Missionaries to North America: Spiritual Writings and Biographical Sketches*, 153.

3 Jean de Brébeuf, "Important Advice for Those Whom it Shall Please God to Call to New France, Especially to the Country of the Hurons," in Roustang, ed., *Jesuit Missionaries to North America: Spiritual Writings and Biographical Sketches*, 141.

4 Reuben Gold Thwaites, ed., *The Jesuit Relations and Allied Documents: Travels and Explorations of the Jesuit Missionairies in New France, 1610-1791*, 71 volumes (Cleveland: The Burrows Brothers, 1897-1901), Vol. 10: 159-61.

5 *The Jesuit Relations*, vol. 15: 77, 97-99.

6 *The Jesuit Relations*, vol. 6: 117.

7 *The Jesuit Relations*, vol. 34: 147.

8 Isaac Jogues, letter to his mother, April 6, 1636, in Roustang, ed., *Jesuit Missionaries to North America: Spiritual Writings and Biographical Sketches*, 223.

9 Isaac Jogues, letter to his mother, June 11, 1637, in Roustang, ed., *Jesuit Missionaries to North America: Spiritual Writings and Biographical Sketches*, 229.

10 Isaac Jogues, letter to his Provincial, August 5, 1643, in Roustang, ed., *Jesuit Missionaries to North America: Spiritual Writings and Biographical Sketches*, 290-91.

11 Isaac Jogues, letter to a fellow Jesuit, September, 1646, in Roustang, ed., *Jesuit Missionaries to North America: Spiritual Writings and Biographical Sketches*, 331.

12 Charles Garnier, letter quoted by Fr. Paul Ragueneau in the *Manuscrit de 1652: Mémoires touchant la mort et les vertus des Pères Isaac Jogues, Anne de Noüe, Antoine Daniel, Jean de Brébeuf, Gabriel Lallemant, Charles Garnier, Noël Chabanel, et un séculier, René Goupil* (Montréal: Archives du Collège Sainte-Marie, n.d.). English translation quoted in Roustang, ed., *Jesuit Missionaries to North America: Spiritual Writings and Biographical Sketches*, 346.

13 Charles Garnier, letter to Reverend Father Ragueneau, December 4, 1649, in Roustang, ed., *Jesuit Missionaries to North America: Spiritual Writings and Biographical Sketches*, 384.

14 Paul Le Jeune, "Relation of 1637," in Reuben Gold Thwaites, ed., *The Jesuit Relations and Allied Documents*, vol. 12: 117.

15 Jean de Brébeuf, "Instructions for the Fathers of Our Society who will be Sent to the Hurons," in Roustang, ed., *Jesuit Missionaries to North America: Spiritual Writings and Biographical Sketches*, 156.

16 Jean de Brébeuf, Letter to the Very Reverend Father Mutius Vitelleschi, General of the Society of Jesus, May 20, 1637; in Reuben Gold Thwaites, ed., *The Jesuit Relations and Allied Documents*, vol. 11: 11.

17 Homily of His Holiness Pope Francis, Eucharistic Celebration at the North American College, Janiculum Hill, Rome, Saturday, 2 May 2015: https://w2.vatican.va/content/francesco/en/homilies/2015/documents/papa-francesco_20150502_omelia-pontifical-north-american-college.html Many students of the history of the California missions have addressed the question of the impact of the history of Serra and his missionary companions on how Americans understand the origins of the nation. See, e.g., Gregory Orfalea, *Journey to the Sun: Junípero Serra's Dream and the Founding of California* (New York: Scribner, 2014), 367, for an account that pits Protestant materialism against Catholic spiritualism. A perhaps more nuanced discussion is found in Robert M. Senkewicz and Rose Marie Beebe, "Serra's Sojourn," Santa Clara Magazine, November 16, 2015: http://magazine.scu.edu/article.cfm?c=23235 where they write that "Serra's voyage from Spain to America reminds us that the growth of

our country has always been more complex than the story offered by the standard 'east to west' narrative, starting with Jamestown and Plymouth Rock." For his part, José H. Gomez, the Archbishop of Los Angeles, himself a Mexican immigrant to the United States, writes that "Father Serra helps us to appreciate in a new way that the missionaries were America's true 'founders.' In him we see that America's origins were not about politics, conquest or plunder. The deepest motives of Father Serra and the missionaries who founded America were religious, spiritual and humanitarian" (Most Reverend José H. Gomez, "Junípero Serra's Mission and America's Religious Foundations and Future," The North American College, Rome, May 2, 2015: http://media.la-archdiocese.org/pope-francis-archbishop-gomez-celebrate-life-and-mission-of-blessed-junipero-serra-at-special-conference-in-rome-2/).

18   Francisco Palóu, *Palóu's Life of Fray Junípero Serra*, ed. and trans. Maynard J. Geiger (Washington, D.C.: Academy of American Franciscan History, 1955), 8.

19   See Steven Turley, *Franciscan Spirituality and Mission in New Spain, 1524-1599* (Farnham: Ashgate Publishing, 2014), 31-33.

20   English translation from Rose Marie Beebe and Robert M. Senkewicz, *Junípero Serra: California, Indians, and the Transformation of a Missionary* (Norman: University of Oklahoma Press, 2015), 63-66. The original (with facing page English translation) is found in Junípero Serra, *Writings of Junípero Serra*, ed. Antonine Tibesar. 4 vols. (Washington, D.C.: Academy of American Franciscan History, 1955-66), vol. 1: 3-9.

21   English translation in Beebe and Senkewicz, op. cit., 197; original in *Writings*, vol. 1: 110-112.

22   Memorandum written by Serra, June 22, 1774; English translation from Beebe and Senkewicz, op. cit., 249; original in Serra, *Writings*, vol. 2: 84-89.

23   See Rubén G. Mendoza, "Presidio Light: A Midwinter Solstice Event at the Presidio Chapel of Santa Bárbara." *La Campana*, Fall 2009. 4-11; and Rubén G. Mendoza, "The Liturgy of Light: Solar Geometry and Kinematic Liturgical Iconography in an Early 19th-Century California Mission." Boletín: *Journal of the California Mission Studies Association*." Vol. 28:1 & 2, 2011 & 2012. 6-21. In addition, see Mendoza's Mission Solstice Survey site at http:// SolsticeChronicles.org .

24   See Beebe and Senkewicz, op. cit., 212-215 for historical background on the origin of the mission system (the creation of congregaciones or reducciones) as an alternative to the military-run encomienda system. Serra's view of the missions as a superior means to assimilate the indigenous populations places him on the "progressive," anti-slavery side of Spanish thinking about colonialism and native populations.

25   English translation in Beebe and Senkewicz, op. cit., 365-369; original in Serra, *Writings*, vol. 3: 406-14.

26   English translation in Beebe and Senkewicz, op. cit., 324, 327, 328; original in Serra, Writings, vol. 2: 400-6.

27   Francisco Palóu, *Relación histórica del Venerable Padre Fray Junípero Serra*, chap. 58; English translation in Beebe and Senkewicz, op. cit., 418, 420.

28   Letter XI, 23 August 1864, in *Life and Letters of Father Damien, The Apostle of the Lepers*. Ed. Fr. Pamphile de Veuster, no translator listed (London: The Catholic Truth Society, 1889), 52-53, translation modified.

29   Quoted in Jan de Volder, *The Spirit of Father Damien: The Leper Priest—A Saint for Our Times* (San Francisco: Ignatius Press, 2010), 20.

30   Ibid., 55-56, translation modified.

31   Quoted in Gavan Daws, *Holy Man: Father Damian of Molokai* (New York: Harper and Row Publishers, 1973), 60.

32   From Letter XVII, 25 November 1873, in *Life and Letters of Father Damien, The Apostle of*

the Lepers, 91-92.

33 Ibid., 92-93.

34 Ibid., 93-94, translation modified.

35 Ibid., Letter XXV, 8 December 1881, 124.

36 Ibid., Letter XXIV, 31 January 1880, 118.

37 Katharine Drexel, Collected Journals, January 1874, quoted in Cheryl C. D. Hughes, *Katharine Drexel: The Riches-to-Rags Life Story of an American Catholic Saint* (Grand Rapids, MI: William. B. Eerdmans Publishing Co., 2014), 54.

38 Katharine Drexel to James O'Connor, August 1885, quoted in Sr. Consuela Marie Duffy, *Katharine Drexel; A Biography* (Philadelphia: P. Reilly Co., 1966), 126.

39 Address at the Catholic Youth Crusade Convention, Dayton, Ohio, 1921, quoted in Duffy, *Katharine Drexel; A Biography*, 100.

40 Katharine Drexel to James O'Connor, 11 November 1888, quoted in Hughes, *Katharine Drexel: The Riches-to-Rags Life*, 93.

41 Katharine Drexel, Letters to the Southwest Missions, 1907, quoted in Hughes, *Katharine Drexel: The Riches-to-Rags Life*, 204.

42 Quoted in Cordelia Frances Biddle, *Saint Katharine: The Life of Katharine Drexel* (Yardley, PA: Westholme Publishing, 2014), 148.

43 Katharine Drexel, Letters to the Sisters of the Blessed Sacrament, July 14, 1905, quoted in Duffy, *Katharine Drexel; A Biography*, 259.

44 Quoted in Duffy, *Katharine Drexel; A Biography*, 239-240.

45 Homily of His Holiness Benedict XVI, Cathedral Square, Erfurt, Saturday, 24 September 2011: https://w2.vatican.va/content/benedict-xvi/en/homilies/2011/documents/hf_ben-xvi_hom_20110924_domplatz-erfurt.html

46 Ibid.—Benedict XVI speaks of saints as those who "catch" Christ's "contagious presence."

47 Jean de Brébeuf, Letter to the Very Reverend Father Mutius Vitelleschi, General of the Society of Jesus, May 20, 1637; in Reuben Gold Thwaites, ed., *The Jesuit Relations and Allied Documents*, vol. 11: 11.

48 Based on Mary Ann Poust, "Returning to Cathedral, Cardinal Encourages Congregation to Give Thanks," *Catholic New York*, November 23, 2006: http://cny.org/stories/Returning-to-Cathedral-Cardinal-Encourages-Congregation-to-Give-Thanks,521?content_source=&category_id=&search_filter=&event_mode=&event_ts_from=&list_type=&order_by=&order_sort=&content_class=&sub_type=stories&town_id=

49 Robert Louis Stevenson, *Father Damien: An Open Letter to the Reverend Doctor Hyde of Honolulu from Robert Louis Stevenson* (Chatto & Windus: London,1890),13-14,15,16, 17.

50 Robert Louis Stevenson, *Father Damien*, 21, 22, 30.

51 T.N. Jagadisan, *Mahatma Gandhi Answers the Challenge of Leprosy* (Madras: no publisher listed, 1965), 3.

52 Homily of His Holiness Pope Benedict XVI, Saint Peter's Square, Sunday, 21 October 2012: http://w2.vatican.va/content/benedict-xvi/en/homilies/2012/documents/hf_ben-xvi_hom_20121021_canonizzazioni.html

53 Homily of His Holiness Pope Francis, National Shrine of the Immaculate Conception, Washington, D.C., Wednesday, 23 September 2015: https://w2.vatican.va/content/francesco/en/homilies/2015/documents/papa-francesco_20150923_usa-omelia-washington-dc.html

54 Homily of His Holiness Benedict XVI, Vatican Basilica, Sunday, 11 October 2009: https://w2.vatican.va/content/benedict-xvi/en/homilies/2009/documents/hf_ben-xvi_hom_20091011_canonizzazioni.html

55 Homily of His Holiness Pope Francis, Cathedral of Sts. Peter and Paul, Philadelphia, Saturday, 26 September 2015: https://w2.vatican.va/content/francesco/en/homilies/2015/

45

documents/papa-francesco_20150926_usa-omelia-philadelphia.html

56 Sources and publications on the shrine of Our Lady of Good Help and the Marian apparitions that occurred there are scarce and limited to informational brochures in English: see E. Looney, *Our Lady of Good Help: Mary's Message and Mission for Adele Brise and the World* (Phoenix: Amor Deus, 2013), and E. Looney, *The Shrine Champion, of Our Lady of Good Help: A Self-Guided Tour* (Phoenix: Amor Deus, 2012); see also L. Winstead, *A Message for Adele* (Create Space Independent Publishing Platform, 2012). The website of the shrine is https://www. shrineofourladyofgoodhelp.com/#demo3

57 Cf. https://web.archive.org/web/20131127041529/ladyofgoodhelp.com/htmPages/g_hst_p2.html

58 https://www.shrineofourladyofgoodhelp.com/shrine/

59 Cf. https://web.archive.org/web/20131127042819/ladyofgoodhelp.com/htmPages/g_hst_p1.html

60 On this famous fire, see D. Gess and W. Lutz, *Firestorm at Peshtigo: A Town, Its People, and the Deadliest Fire in American History* (New York: Holt Paperbacks, 2003), and P. Pernin, *The Great Peshtigo Fire: An Eyewitness Account* (Madison: Wisconsin Historical Society Press, 1999).

61 The Congregation of the Missionary Fathers of Mercy has as its main goal the preaching of retreats for parishes, focusing especially on the importance of the Eucharist and Confession. The order was founded by Jean-Baptiste Rauzan in 1808 under the name "Missionaries of France," with the purpose of re-evangelizing post-revolutionary France. Today the order is only present in the United States, and its headquarters are located just a few miles from Bowling Green, Kentucky.

62 Ecclesiastical approval took many years due to a lack of rigorous research about the apparitions, as well as the very particular, local nature of the devotion. The decree which approves the apparitions describes the steps taken for reaching such approval, which is based on the little written evidence that remains, as well as a century-old tradition of popular devotion. The full text of the decree of approval can be found on the official website of the shrine. On the ecclesiastical norms concerning the discernment of apparitions and private revelations, see Sacred Congregation for the Doctrine of Faith, "Norms Regarding the Manner of Proceeding in the Discernment of Presumed Apparitions or Revelations, Preliminary Note," 25 February 1978 (available on the Vatican website, www.vatican.va); see also R. Laurentin, *Dizionario delle "apparizioni" della Vergine Maria* (Rome: ART, 2010); A. Grasso, *Perché appare la Madonna? Per capire le apparizioni mariane* (Conegliano: Ancilla, 2010).

63 G. Grant, *Technology and Empire: Perspectives on North America, in Collected Works*, vol. 3 (Toronto: University of Toronto Press, 2005), 490.

CPSIA information can be obtained
at www.ICGtesting.com
Printed in the USA
FSOW03n0627301217
42552FS

9 781941 457047